Jaguars

By Pat Lalley

Steadwell Books

Raintree Steck-Vaughn Publishers

A Harcourt Company

Austin · New York
www.steck-vaughn.com

ANIMALS OF THE RAIN FOREST

Published by Raintree Steck-Vaughn Publishers, an imprint of Steck-Vaughn Company.

Library of Congress Cataloging-in-Publication Data
Lalley, Pat.
    Jaguars/by Pat Lalley.
        p.cm.--(Animals of the rain forest)
    Includes index.
    ISBN 0-7398-3102-X
    1. Jaguars--Juvenile literature. [1. Jaguars.] I. Title. II. Series
QL737.C23 L35 2000
599.75'5--dc21

00-033816

Printed in the United States of America
10 9 8 7 6 5 4 3 2 1 LB 02 01 00

Produced by Compass Books

Photo Acknowledgments
Archive Photos, 22
Henry Doorly Zoo, Cover, 24
Photo Network/Mark Newman, 12, 14, 27
Smithsonian Institute, 4–5
Visuals Unlimited/Mark Newman, 8; James Beveridge, 11, 16, 18;
    William Grenfel, 20; Joe Mcdonald, 29

Content Consultant
Liz Harmon
Animal Curator
Henry Doorly Zoo, Omaha, Nebraska

Contents

Range of the Jaguar

MEXICO

BELIZE

HONDURAS

GUATEMALA

NICARAGUA *Caribbean Sea*

EL SALVADOR

COSTA RICA

PANAMA

VENEZUELA

COLOMBIA

ECUADOR

PERU

AMAZON RIVER

BRAZIL

BOLIVIA

South Pacific Ocean

CHILE

PARAGUAY

URUGUAY

ARGENTINA

GUYANA

SURINAME

FRENCH GUIANA (FRANCE)

North Atlantic Ocean

South Atlantic Ocean

A Quick Look at Jaguars

What do jaguars look like?
Jaguars are the third largest
cat in the world. They have
light yellow, red-brown, or
pure black fur with black spots
called rosettes.

Where do jaguars live?
Jaguars live in South America, Central America,
and southern Mexico. They live in forests, rain
forests, mountains, and large grasslands called
savannahs.

What do jaguars eat?
Jaguars are carnivores. They eat only other
animals, such as wild pigs, cattle, and deer.

Do jaguars have any enemies?
Jaguars have few enemies. Caimans or
anacondas will sometimes eat young jaguars.
But humans are the biggest threat to these cats.
Jaguars are an endangered species. They are in
danger of dying out.

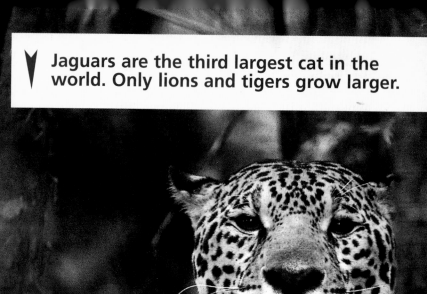
Jaguars are the third largest cat in the world. Only lions and tigers grow larger.

Jaguars in the Rain Forest

The jaguar is the largest cat living in North, Central, and South America. Large jaguars are about 2.5 feet (1 m) tall at the shoulders. They are 5 feet (1.5 m) long or more. They weigh up to 250 pounds (113 kg).

A jaguar's coat is soft and woolly. Its hairs are short and smooth. Jaguars' throats and undersides are usually white. Their bodies can be light yellow, red-brown, or pure black. Most jaguars are yellow.

All jaguars have black spots called rosettes. A rosette is a ringlike spot with smaller spots inside it. A row of rosettes in the middle of some jaguars' backs may look like a thick black line. Rosettes are hard to see on black jaguars. The spots blend in with the dark fur.

Where Jaguars Live

Most wild jaguars live in and around the rain forests of Central and South America. Some live in southern Mexico. Jaguars live in many types of habitats. A habitat is a place where an animal or plant usually lives and grows. Jaguars can live in rain forests, mountains, and large grasslands called savannahs.

Most wild jaguars live in Amazonia. This is the largest rain forest in the world. It grows around the banks of the Amazon River. The thick forest has many hiding places for these big cats. They can find water and food easily.

Unlike most cats, jaguars spend a lot of time in the water. They may spend half of their day in streams or rivers. Water helps them keep cool in the hot rain forest. Jaguars often hunt in water, too.

Territories

A jaguar needs many miles of territory to look for food. A territory is a space the jaguar knows well. It lives and hunts in its territory.

 A jaguar might fight other jaguars to protect its territory.

Jaguars put markers around their territories. They scratch trees. They also put their scents, or odors around their territories. These markers tell other animals that the territory is taken.

A jaguar's territory usually includes water. The cat swims in the water to travel around its territory, stay cool, drink, and hunt.

Jaguars sink two, long teeth called fangs into animals' skin to catch and hold them.

Special Body Parts

Jaguars have large heads and sharp teeth. Their jaws are the strongest of all the big cats. Jaguar bites can break the skulls of other animals. A skull is the bone inside the head that protects the brain.

Jaguars' paws are made for hunting. A soft pad covers each foot. The pads help a jaguar walk quietly over any kind of land. This helps the jaguar sneak up on other animals.

Claws serve many uses. Jaguars use claws to climb trees. Their claws help them catch prey. Prey are the animals that jaguars hunt and eat.

Jaguars have retractable claws. Retractable means able to pull back in. They pull their claws back inside their paws when they walk or run. This helps them go faster to chase prey.

Jaguars push out their claws once they have found prey. Their claws help jaguars catch and hold the struggling animals. Jaguars sometimes use their claws to kill the animals they eat.

Jaguars use their sharp claws to climb trees to look for prey.

Hunting and Eating

Jaguars are predators. They hunt and catch other animals. Jaguars eat more than 80 kinds of prey.

Jaguars hunt mainly small animals. They often eat rodents. Rodents are small animals with two large front teeth. Capybaras are an important food for jaguars. These are the world's largest rodents. They are 2 feet (.6 m) tall. They weigh about 100 pounds (45 kg). Jaguars sometimes kill large animals, such as horses or cattle.

Jaguars are excellent swimmers. They catch many animals that live in the water. Jaguars are also very good climbers. They use their claws to climb tall trees to catch prey, such as birds.

Jaguars often hunt along animal trails in the rain forest.

Eating Often

Jaguars need to eat often because they move around a great deal. Sometimes jaguars eat large animals, such as deer. A big meal may last a jaguar several days. But large animals are hard to catch and kill. They often outrun or fight jaguars.

South American Indians named jaguars for the way the cats kill. The word jaguar means "beast that kills its prey with one bound."

Jaguars eat small animals if they cannot catch large ones. But small animals do not keep a jaguar full for long. Jaguars must catch food almost every day if they eat only small animals.

Night Hunters

Jaguars hunt mainly at night. They can see well in the dark. They can see six times better than people can. Jaguars are good hunters because they can see well. They can see prey that is hiding in the rain forest, even at night.

But it is hard for prey to see jaguars. The color and spots of these cats help them blend into the rain forest. This helps them hide in plants and sneak up on other animals. Black jaguars can easily hide at night. Their black coats make them blend in with the darkness.

Jaguars swim in the river to catch fish, turtles, and animals that are drinking at the water's edge.

Hunting

Jaguars often stalk their prey. Stalk means they track and follow prey for miles. They attack when their prey least expects it. This way of hunting makes prey easier to catch.

Jaguars often hunt along animal trails in the rain forest. They have a better chance of finding and catching prey on trails. Jaguars may stalk their prey for awhile or attack it right away.

Jaguars also hunt for fish or turtles in water. Sometimes jaguars hide near water. They wait for birds and other animals to come drink the water. Then jaguars quickly jump on their prey.

Jaguars slap with their paws to kill smaller animals. They slap an animal's head, which breaks the animal's skull. People have seen jaguars kill dogs this way.

Jaguars use their jaws to kill large animals. Jaguars kill with one strong bite behind the ears of prey. This bite breaks the prey's skulls. Other big cats kill by biting the necks of prey.

Jaguars spend most of their lives alone. They spend time together only during mating season.

A Jaguar's Life Cycle

Jaguars live alone. The only time they come together is to mate. Jaguars can mate at any time during the year. But they must first find mates. This is not always easy in huge rain forests and savannahs.

Jaguars find mates by roaring. They give a series of special mating calls. Other jaguars hear the roars. They travel until they find each other.

Female jaguars also mark their territories with special scents. The scents tell male jaguars that the females are ready to mate. Male jaguars can smell the scents. They follow the scents to find female mates.

Jaguar pairs leave each other after mating. The male jaguar does not help raise its young.

Finding Dens

The female jaguar finds a den after mating. A den is a hidden place where she can give birth safely. The female looks for a den on high ground away from rivers. This way, the den will not flood during heavy rain.

A female jaguar gives birth about three months after mating. She has from two to four young.

Female jaguars take care of their cubs for up to two years.

Cubs

Young jaguars are called cubs. Each cub weighs about 2 pounds (.9 kg). At first, cubs are blind because their eyes are closed. Their eyes open in about two weeks.

Cubs live in the den for six months. For three months, they drink their mother's milk. Then they hunt with their mother. Their mother teaches them how to stalk and kill prey.

Cubs do not grow to full size for two years. Young jaguars stay with their mothers until they are fully grown.

Full-grown jaguars leave their mothers. They find their own territories. They hunt, eat, and live alone.

Wild jaguars live 10 to 12 years. Jaguars in zoos live 20 years or more.

Living with Jaguars

The jaguar is special to many South American Indians. For them, the animal means strength.

The Tucano Indians believe the roar of the jaguar is the sound of thunder. The Maya Indians believe the cat is a god.

Some American Indians told stories called myths to explain things in nature. One Indian myth tells how the jaguar got its spots. It says the jaguar put mud on its body with its paws.

◀ **Some Indians in Amazonia study how the jaguar hunts. They try to hunt like the jaguar does.**

A Popular Cat

People in many parts of the world believe jaguars are strong and beautiful. Some companies use the name and the picture of the jaguar. Companies want people to believe the things they make and sell are strong, fast, and beautiful.

A car company in England is named after the big cat. Most of the cars have a small silver jaguar ornament on their hoods.

Some sports teams use jaguars as mascots. A mascot is a symbol for a group. One of these teams is the Jacksonville Jaguars. This National Football League team plays its home games in Jacksonville, Florida. The Jaguars is one of the newest professional football teams in the United States.

People use pictures of black jaguars in commercials, movies, and TV shows to help sell things. You can see the rosettes of this black jaguar on the top of its head.

Jaguars in Danger

Jaguars have few enemies in the rain forest. Sometimes anacondas or caimans will kill young jaguars, but this does not happen often. A caiman is a kind of crocodile.

People are jaguars' main enemy. People hunt the cats for their fur. They use fur to make coats and other clothing. In the 1960s and 1970s, about 18,000 jaguars were killed every year for their fur. There are only about 15,000 jaguars left in the wild.

Another danger to jaguars is the loss of the rain forest. Governments are tearing down rain forests to make farms and houses for people. Jaguars live, hunt, eat, and have young in the rain forest. Jaguars cannot live in the wild without their rain forest homes.

Today, it is against the law to hunt jaguars in some South and Central American countries. But the cats are still an endangered species. An endangered species is one that is close to dying out forever. It is against the law to buy and sell the cats or their fur in the United States.

▲ **It is against the law to hunt jaguars in wildlife parks.**

Some people want to protect jaguars. They have tried to pass more laws against hunting and have started wildlife parks. Jaguars in these parks are kept safe from hunters. The country of Belize in Central America started a park to save jaguars. About 200 jaguars live in the Cockscomb Basin Wildlife Sanctuary and Jaguar Preserve. More jaguars live in this park than anywhere outside of Amazonia.

Glossary

Amazonia (am-uh-ZONE-ee-uh)—the largest rain forest in the world

carnivore (KARN-i-vor)—an animal that only eats other animals

mascot (MA-scot)—a symbol for a group

myth (MYTH)—a story told to explain something in nature

predator (PRED-uh-tur)—an animal that hunts and eats other animals

prey (PRAY)—animals that are hunted by other animals for food

rainy season (RAY-nee SEE-suhn)—a time of several months when it rains almost every day in the rain forest; forests and grasslands flood during the rainy season.

rosette (roh-SET)—a ringlike spot with smaller spots inside it

savannah (suh-VAN-uh)—a flat, grassy plain with few or no trees

stalk (STAUK)—to secretly track and follow prey

Internet Sites and Addresses

Cockscomb Basin Wildlife Sanctuary and Jaguar Preserve
http://ambergriscaye.com/pages/town/
parkcockscomb.html

Lioncrusher's Domain—Jaguar
http://www.geocities.com/RainForest/Vines/8591
/bigcats/jaguar.htm

The Wild Ones—Jaguar
http://www.thewildones.org/Belize/jaguar.html

Rain Forest Action Network
221 Pine Street, Suite 500
San Francisco, CA 94104

World Wildlife Fund
1250 Twenty-fourth Street NW
Washington, DC 20037

Index